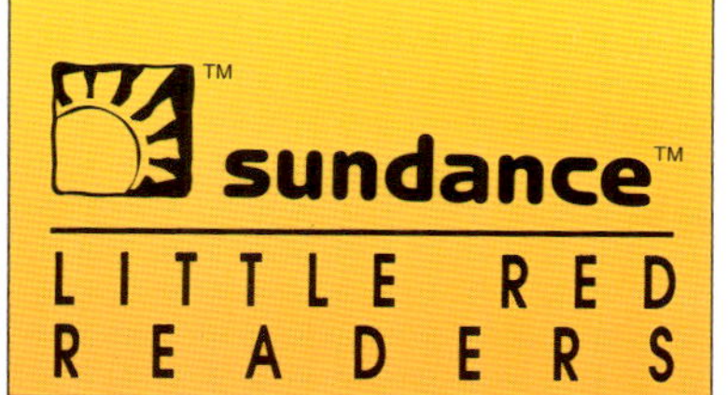

Animal Noises

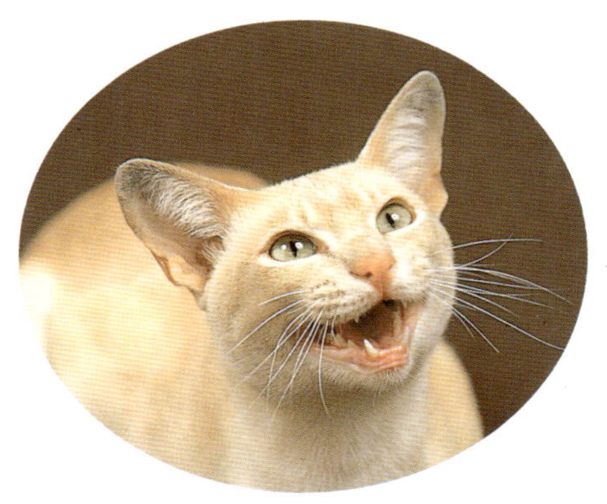

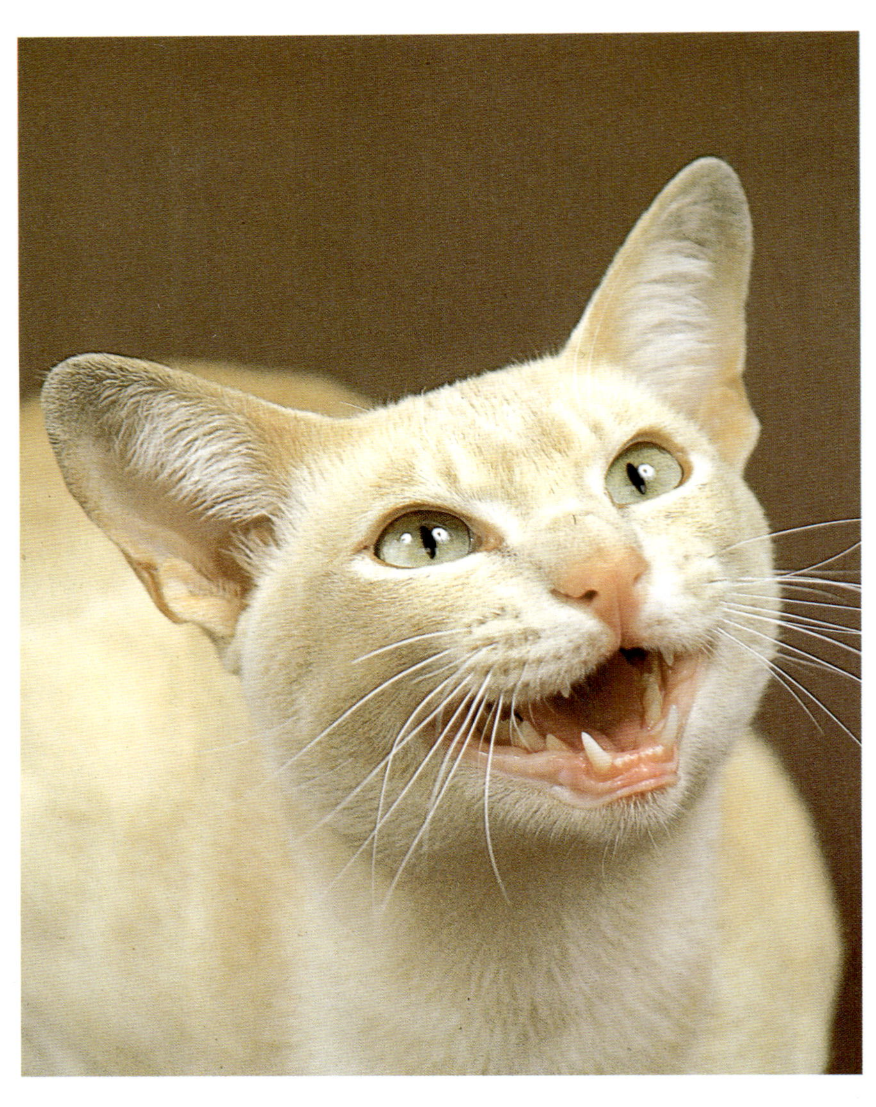

This is a cat.
A cat can meow.

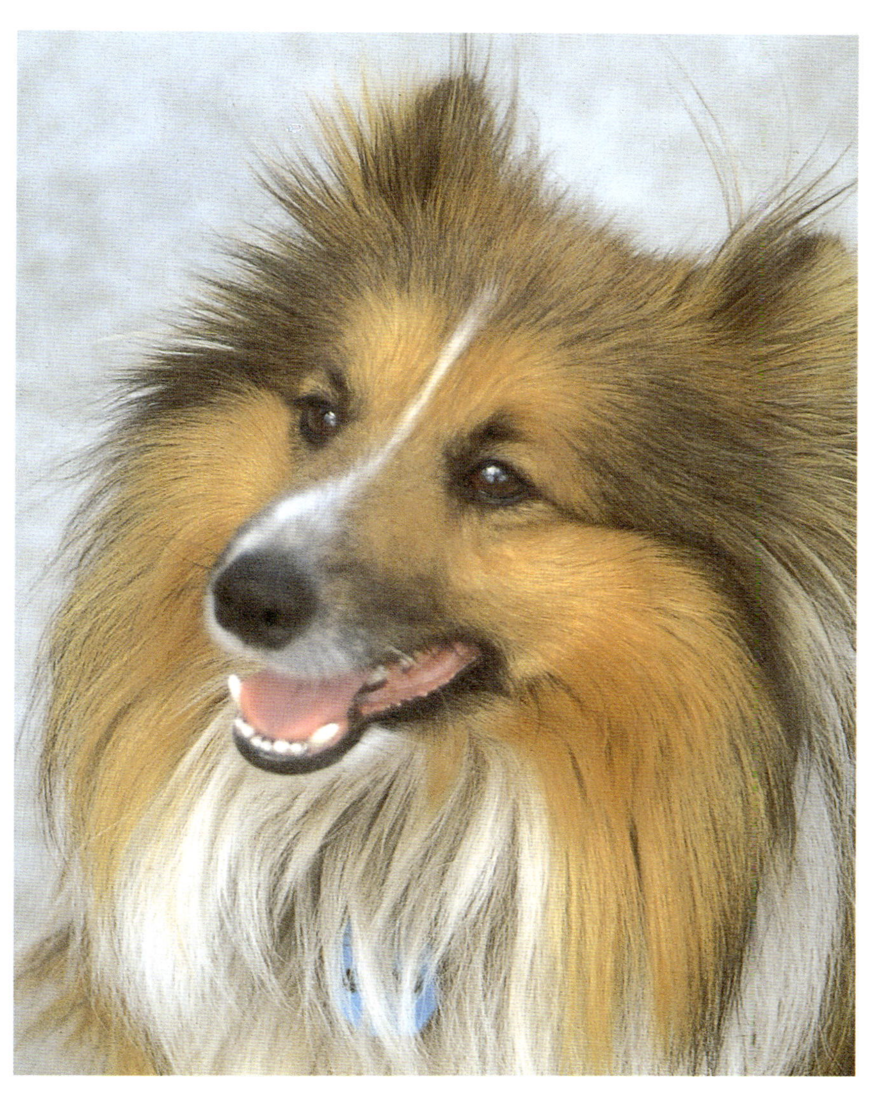

This is a dog.
A dog can bark.

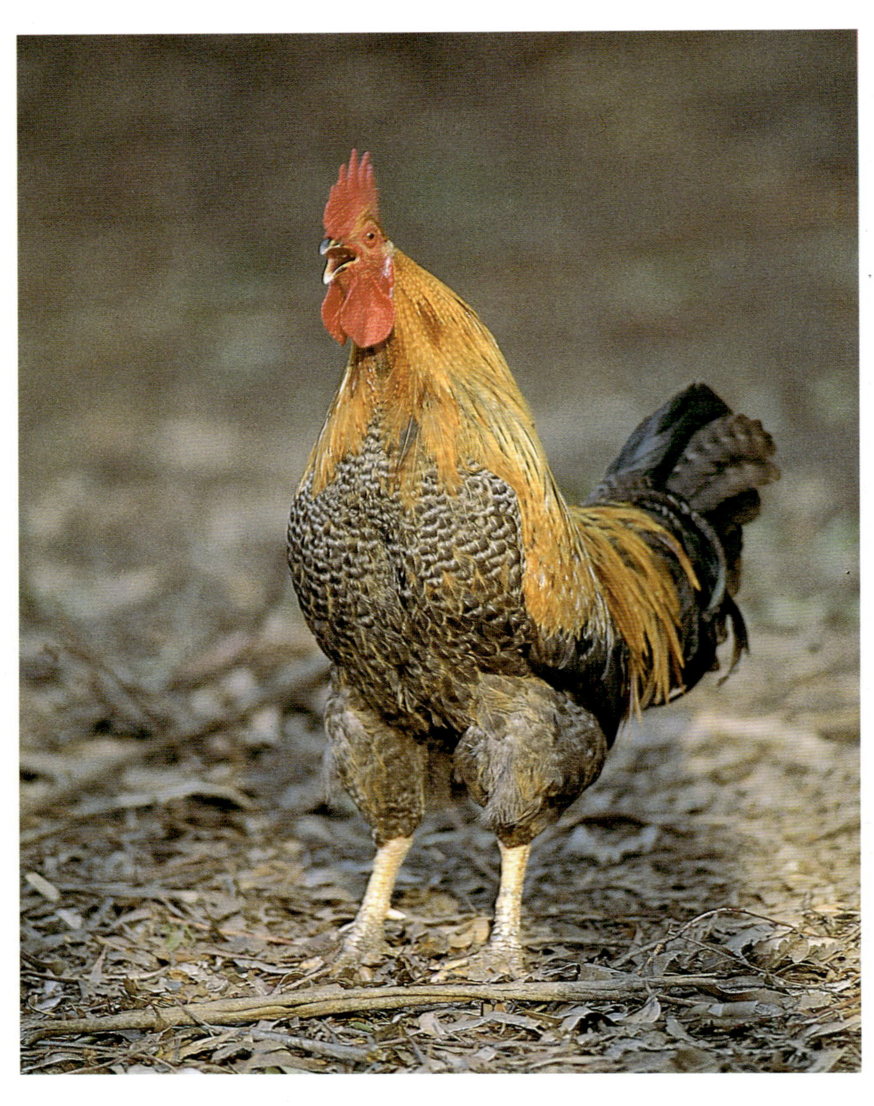

This is a rooster.
A rooster can crow.

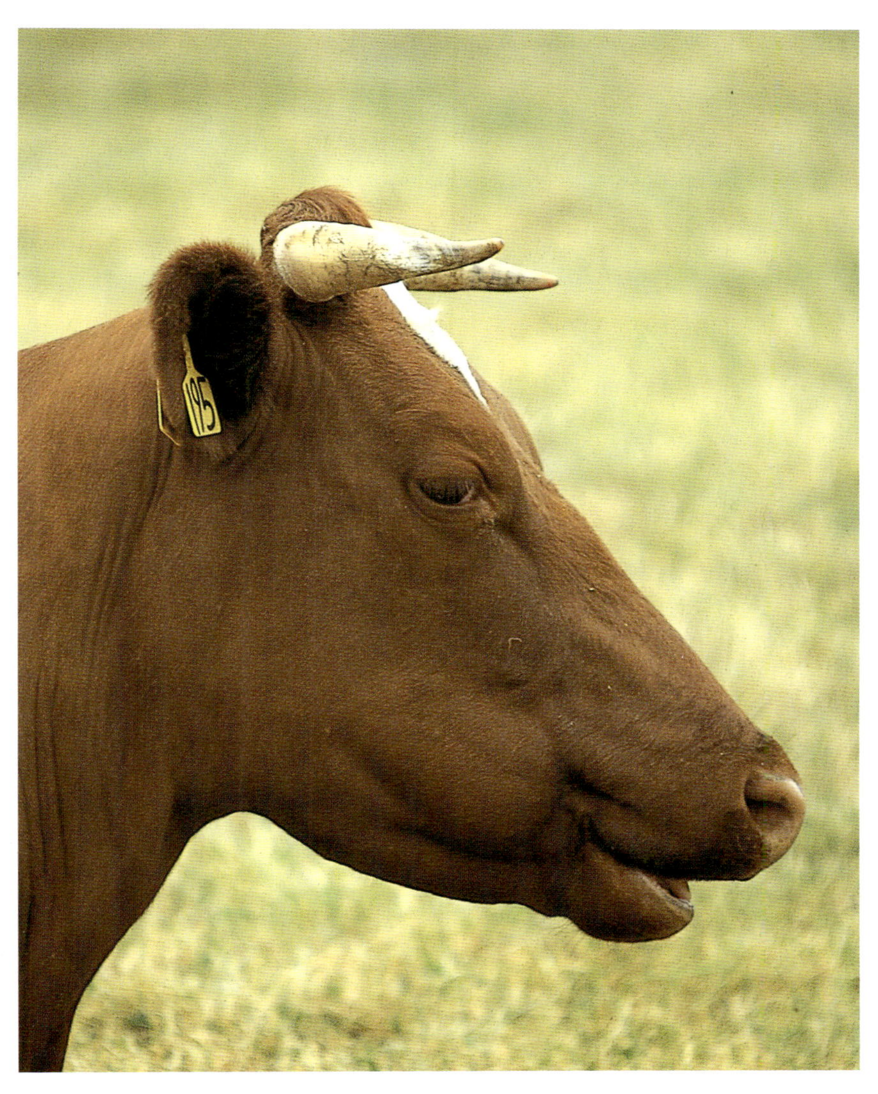

This is a cow.
A cow can moo.

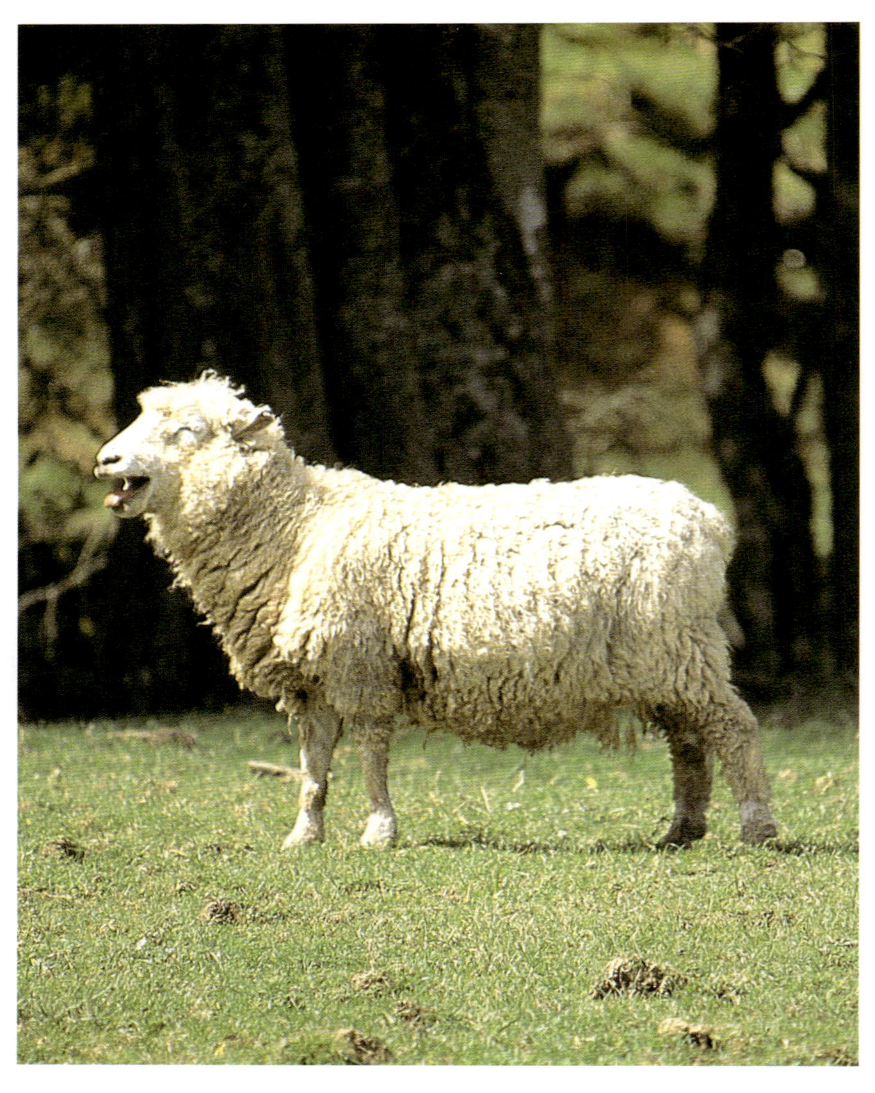

This is a sheep.
A sheep can bleat.

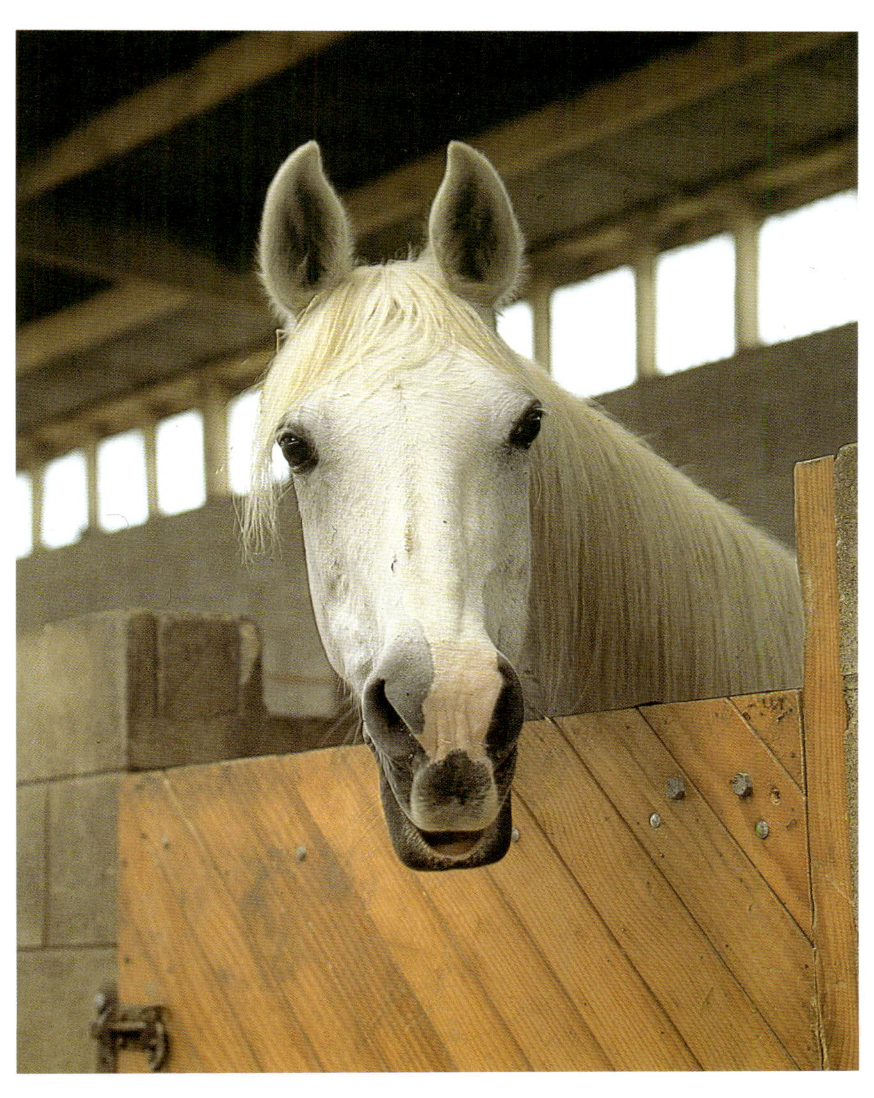

This is a horse.
A horse can neigh.

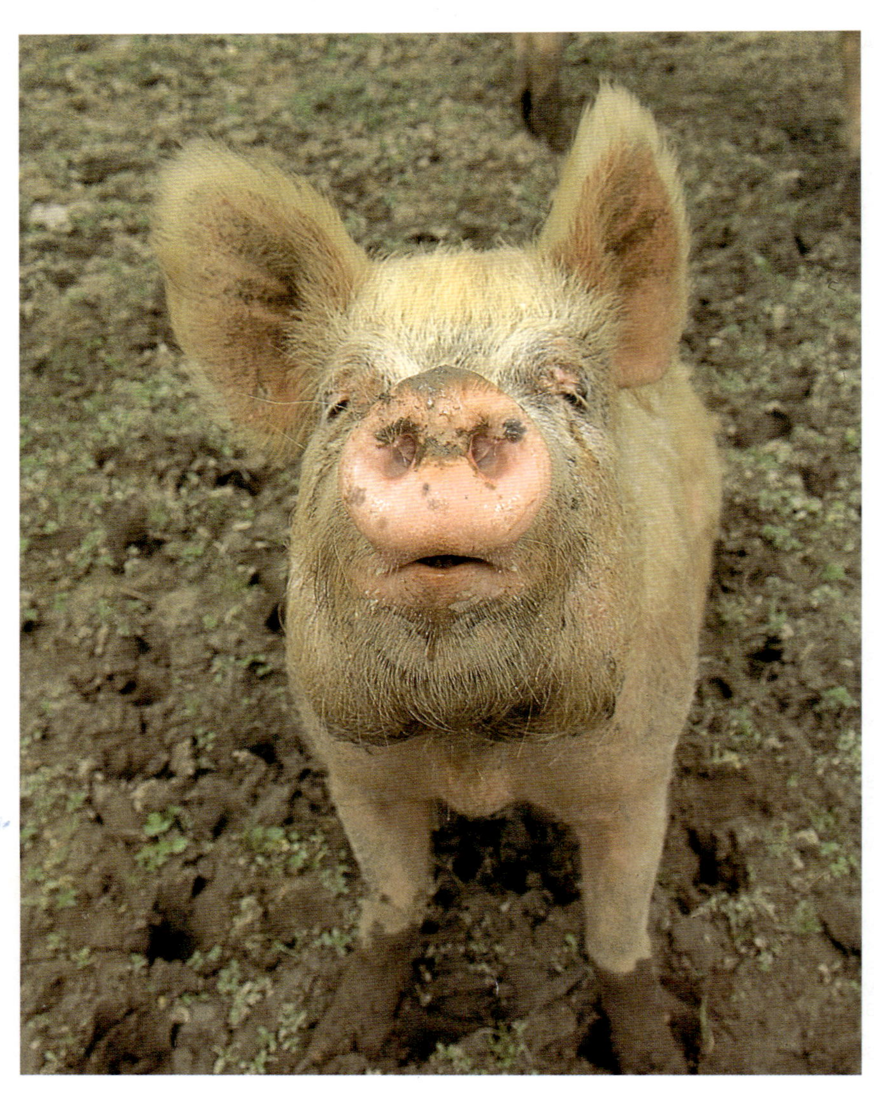

This is a pig.
A pig can oink.

8